Letter to a
Theistic
Evolutionist

Duane T. Gish

ICON
PUBLISHING GROUP

Letter to a
Theistic
Evolutionist

Sincerely,

your brother

in Christ,

Duane T. Gish, PhD.

First printing: March 2012

Icon Publishing
Customer Service: +1 877 887 0222
P.O. Box 2180
Noble, OK 73068
ISBN: 978-1-933267-23-4

Cover and Interior by Brent Spurlock, Green Forest, AR

Printed in the United States of America

Please visit our website for other great titles:
www.iconpublishinggroup.com

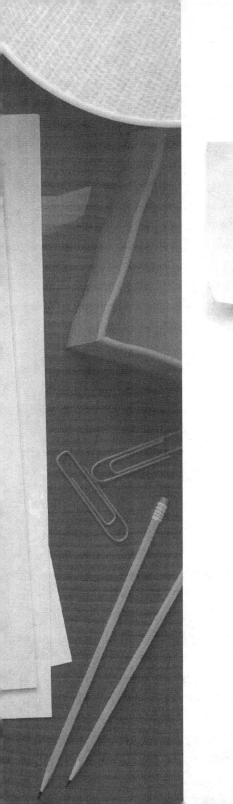

Table of Contents

7

Foreword

This "Letter to a Theistic Evolutionist" by Duane Gish is one of the longest letters I have ever read, but it is wonderfully typical of the thoroughness and competence of my esteemed friend and long-time colleague. When he undertakes an assignment—even a self-imposed assignment—he does it masterfully and completely.

There has been a significant revival of sound Biblical and scientific creationism during the last several decades. Numerous books have been published in this period by creationist scientists and others but the incisive summary of the evidence against evolution in this small book is so compelling that I cannot see how any theistic evolutionist could continue to believe in evolution after reading it. With his some 300 scientific debates against evolutionary scientists plus countless lectures all over the world, Dr. Gish has been one of the main reasons for that revival of creationism—especially of what can be called creation science, the study of scientific evidences for creation and against evolution.

It has been my great privilege to work closely with Dr. Gish in our Institute for Creation Research for almost 35 years—and for several years before that on the board of the Creation Research Society. He is a true scientist, with seemingly encyclopedic knowledge of the scientific evidence relevant to origins, especially in his own specialization (biochemistry) and also in paleontology, astronomy and every other science that has relevance to the vital issue of origins.

Furthermore, he is a Christian gentleman in the finest sense, active in church and school ministry, patient and courteous in debate, beloved by family and colleagues, liked and respected even by his evolutionist adversaries.

This "letter" to Dr. Stephen Godfrey has become a unique sort of book. In the process of replying to Dr. Godfrey's original request, his letter kept growing and growing, incorporating such extensive pertinent documentation, that it eventually "evolved" (pardon the expression!) into this very readable and convincing book on the fallacies of evolution.

I hope that Dr. Godfrey will read it carefully and with open heart, but also that many other young men and women who have gone through similar experiences like his will be freed from their impossible search for a way to accommodate evolutionism with Biblical Christianity. Our Bible has stood every test and is the inspired, inerrant Word of the living God. It abundantly satisfies both heart and mind when accepted as such by His children.

Duane Gish—his life and testimony—is himself a great witness to what God can do with a man firmly committed to Christ and His Word. "*For the eyes of the LORD run to and fro throughout the whole earth, to shew Himself strong in the behalf of them whose heart is perfect toward Him*" (II Chronicles 16:9).

I believe that our Lord found such a man in Dr. Duane Gish! I know you will enjoy and profit from reading this book.

– Henry M. Morris

Introduction

In May of 2005 I received a copy of the book *Paradigms on Pilgrimage: Creationism, Paleontology, and Biblical Interpretation*, by Stephen J. Godfrey and Christopher R. Smith. The book was sent to me by Dr. Godfrey with the request that I examine the information attributed to me in the book and let them know if that information is accurate or if there is something that needed to be corrected. After noting that nothing really needed to be changed, I proceeded to read the book carefully, recording notes on its contents. I felt so strongly alienated by the views expressed by the authors that I decided to write a critique of these views to send to Godfrey and Smith. The "letter" turned out to be much longer than I had intended, even though much more could have been written. I gave copies to several of my fellow scientists at the Institute for Creation Research. Both Dr. Henry Morris and Dr. John Morris suggested that I should consider publishing my comments to Drs. Godfrey and Smith in book form. This little book is the result.

Dr. Godfrey, who describes his field as that of a descriptive paleontologist, received his Ph.D. from McGill University and is now the Curator of Paleontology at the Calvert Marine Museum in Solomons, Maryland. Dr. Christopher R. Smith, who is now pastor of the University Baptist Church in East Lansing Michigan (the home of Michigan State University), received his Ph.D. from Boston College.

Godfrey describes his early years in a family where the Genesis account of creation was accepted literally, and the theory of evolution was equated to man's attempt to deny the existence of God. At that time and later during his early years at the university, Godfrey accepted and defended Biblical creation. He soon, however, began to have some doubts. One of his earliest problems was how to account for the existence of carnivores, or meat-eating creatures. He relates the fact that he attended a seminar at which I spoke in Montreal, Quebec. He mentioned that during "one of our corridor conversations" Gish had suggested that "many organisms may have been converted from herbivory to carnivory by God when Adam and Eve sinned," but that I had admitted that the Bible was silent on this matter. Yes, the Bible is silent on this matter. It has been many years since that conversation, thus neither of us could be certain just exactly what was said. Actually, my explanation that I give now and most likely what I gave then was that since God knew that man was going to sin and the world was to be cursed by all sorts of violence, including creatures eating other creatures, God had equipped many creatures with defense mechanisms. Those creatures that were equipped with features initially designed for the consumption of fruits and plants but which coincidentally could also adapt to capturing and eating prey and who had a desire to do so, began to eat meat.

During his last years at Bishop's University Godfrey relates the fact that he had decided to study vertebrate paleontology in graduate school in order to find out if the paleontological evidence was reliable. He honestly believed that he might find evidence that would bolster the creationist position. This was critical, he says, because his confidence in the reliability of the Christian faith rested at that time on his acceptance of a literal reading of the Genesis creation account. What he failed to recognize then and fails to recognize now was that in attending secular universities, such as McGill University, he was exposing himself to interpretations of the history of life as found in the fossil record by evolutionists, almost all of whom were non-Christians, and most of whom had no use for the Biblical record of creation, or anything else Christian, for that matter. He did recognize then, he said, that if the Bible were inaccurate on natural-scientific matters, on what basis was he to accept its divine authority on matters of morality? Actually, this is the reason today why, having been convinced by the education they receive in our secular schools and universities, a large percentage of our young people reject Biblical truths, including its authority on matters of morality.

He early encountered evidence, he relates, that challenged his creationist beliefs. First was based on the fossil bird, *Archaeopteryx*, the anatomy of which, he was taught, was more similar to the dinosaur, *Compsognathus*, than it was to other birds. *Archaeopteryx* was a bird that possessed perching feet, the basic form and pattern of the avian wing, feathers identical to the feathers of modern birds, a bird-like skull, and the 2-3-4 pattern of digits of birds (dinosaur digits are the 1-2-3 digits). *Compsognathus* was a lizard-hipped dinosaur, not a bird-hipped dinosaur, and possessed none of the features mentioned above for *Archaeopteryx*. Dr. Alan Feduccia, an evolutionist and ornithologist (expert on birds) has pointed out that paleontologists have misinterpreted a significant number of features of *Archaeopteryx*. Although, as an evolutionist, Feduccia believes that birds had evolved from some sort of a reptile, he, along with other ornithologists, maintains that birds did not evolve from dinosaurs.

Archaeopteryx

Feduccia states that "*Archaeopteryx* probably cannot tell us much about the early origins of feathers and flight in true protobirds because *Archaeopteryx* was, in a modern sense, a bird."[1] Larry Martin, an ornithologist at Kansas University, states that "The theory linking dinosaurs to birds is a pleasant fantasy, that some scientists like because it provides a direct entry into a past that we otherwise can

1. *Science* 259:792, 1993

only guess about."[2] If what Martin says is true, then early in his search for truth, Godfrey's search led him to accept a pleasant fantasy.

Another jolt to his belief in creation at Bishop's University was the challenge to Godfrey by a faculty member to explain the multiple fossilized forest layers at Joggins, Nova Scotia, Canada. These are allegedly a series of fossilized forests, buried successively over some millions of years of time. Godfrey originally had accepted young earth creationism. The question of these "fossilized forests" is discussed in the text. Later, Godfrey characterizes research on fossil tracks as the final nails in the coffin of flood geology. From then on it was not only complete acceptance of evolutionary uniformitarian geology and the notion that the flood of Noah was merely a local flood, but the total acceptance of biological evolution, including the evolutionary origin of man. Godfrey and Smith tell us that Genesis, chapters 1-11, is not literal history at all but must be viewed as poetry. He had assistance in accepting this view from his brother-in-law, Christopher Smith, who apparently had been taught this in the seminary where he had received his theological training.

---

2. *Sunday World-Herald*, Omaha, NB. Jan. 19, 1992, p. 17B

In my letter to Godfrey I describe the evidence that leads me to totally reject their interpretation of both the Bible and the scientific evidence related to origins. Certainly much more could be written that would assist in establishing the historicity of Genesis and which would provide additional evidence for the literal creation of the universe and all living creatures by God as described in Genesis.

It would be good for the readers of this book to obtain a copy of the book by Godfrey and Smith so that they would have a complete record of the arguments of these authors. The book may be obtained from Clements Publishing, Toronto, Canada. www.clementspublishing.com. The address is:

6021 Yonge Street
Suite 213
Toronto, Ontario
M2M 3W2 Canada
Tel: 416-558-9439
Fax: 416-352-5997
E-mail: info@clementspublishing.com

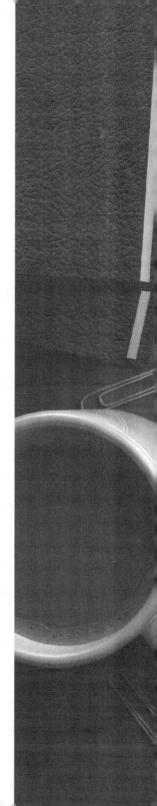

October 31, 2005

Dr. Stephen Godfrey
2710 Hatteras Lane
Lusby, MD 20657

Dear Brother Godfrey:

As one who professes faith in the truth that Jesus Christ is the Son of God who shed his blood for our sins on the cross as described in the Bible, I accept you as a truly born again Christian brother. However, as one who believes that God had the ability to communicate with the humans He created in a way we could know what He meant to tell us, I am distressed by your conversion to the current evolutionary paradigm that is without exception accepted by atheists and other philosophical materialists, and that you have consigned most of the Bible, especially the first eleven chapters of Genesis, which contain all of the fundamentals of our Christian faith, to poetry rather than to a true historical account. I have spent hours reading your book and have made twelve pages of notes, and much more could have been written. First, I will answer your request that I indicate whether I find your references to me to be satisfactory. Just one reference I do find to be untrue. On page 75, you write, "...Stephen Jay Gould described some of the courtroom 'debates' that he had had with Duane T. Gish and other young-earth creationists." I was in only one courtroom with Gould, and that was in Little Rock, Arkansas, during the 1981 Federal trial of the equal time creation/evolution law passed by the Arkansas legislature. I did not speak with him at all at that time. In fact I have never had a single conversation with him at any time. What you have here is of course Gould's statement and not one of your own. Don't bother to change it. The editor of *Discover* did allow me to write a one-page reply to an article by Gould[1] in which he supported evolution and attacked creationists, including me personally (I had asked the editor to allow me to publish an article of equal length to that of Gould, but he refused). Gould attacked me in his article for stating that Richard Goldschmidt believed that the first bird hatched from a reptilian egg. In my reply I quoted Goldschmidt's statement in

1. *Discover*, May 1981, p.37

one of his books that the first bird did hatch from a reptilian egg. In his rebuttal to my article, Gould claimed once more that Goldschmidt believed no such thing and that he had merely used a metaphor. Ernst Mayr, seven years later in his 1988 book, *Toward a New Philosophy of Biology*, pp 65-67, said that:

> Gould (1982) is also wrong in claiming that Goldschmidt never had the view 'that new species arise all at once, fully formed, by a fortunate macromutation.' Actually, this is what Goldschmidt repeatedly claimed. For instance, he cited with approval Schindewolfe's suggestion that the first bird hatched out of a reptilian egg, and was even clearer on this point in a later paper[2] than in his 1940 book.

I am sure, by the way, that Mayr had no knowledge of my exchange with Gould on that point. We can see that it was Gould who misquoted Goldschmidt, not me.

In your approach to the question of origins you attempt to separate methodological naturalism, which does not admit

2. 1952:91-92

supernatural causes as it seeks to explain the phenomena it is observing, from metaphysical naturalism. This we can do (I can think of a possible exception which I will discuss later) when we are attempting to observe, understand, and explain the **operation** of the universe and its living organisms. In fact, this is the only way scientists can operate. We assume the universe and living organisms operate according to natural laws and processes which creationists believe were instituted by God... However, evolutionists step outside of empirical science when they insist that we must use these same natural laws and processes to explain the **origin** of the universe and living organisms. There were no human witnesses to the origin of the universe, the origin of life, or the origin of a single living thing. These events took place in the unobservable past and are not repeatable in the present. Today we observe only variations within species, accepted by both creationists and evolutionists, but we don't see apes changing into humans or any macroevolutionary changes postulated by evolutionists. Neither creation nor evolution is a scientific theory. They are theories about history and theories about history are not scientific theories. They are inferences based on circumstantial evidence. We do have circumstantial evidence to compare the claims based on each theory, and it seems obvious that one or the other must be true.

To substantiate my claim that evolution is not a scientific theory I quote evolutionary biologists Paul Ehrlich and L. C. Birch,

> Our theory of evolution has become...one which cannot be refuted by any possible observations. Every conceivable observation can be fitted into it. It is thus 'outside of empirical science' but not necessarily false. No one can think of ways to test it. Ideas, either without basis or based on a few laboratory experiments carried out in extremely simplified systems have attained currency far beyond their validity. They have become part of an evolutionary dogma accepted by most of us as part of our training.[3]

Obviously, any theory outside of empirical science and which has no way to be tested is not a scientific theory. Evolutionary theory has become so plastic it doesn't make

---

3. *Nature* 214:352, 1967

any difference what the data are. Theodosius Dobzhansky has said that:

> Those evolutionary happenings are unique, unrepeatable, and irreversible. It is as impossible to turn a land vertebrate into a fish as it is to effect the reverse transformation. The applicability of the experimental method to the study of such unique historical processes is severely restricted before all else by the time intervals involved, which far exceed the lifetime of any human experimenter. And yet it is just such impossibility that is demanded by anti-evolutionists when they ask for "proofs" of evolution which they would magnanimously accept as satisfactory.[4]

Dobzhansky and evolutionists demand that creation be excluded from consideration because the applicability of the experimental method cannot be applied to creation, but he admits that the applicability of the experimental method

---

4. *American Scientist* 45:388, 1957

to evolutionary theory is likewise impossible. Bryan Apple-
yard has stated that:

> (Evolution) must, they feel, explain every-
> thing...A theory that explains everything
> might just as well be discarded since it has
> no real explanatory value. Of course, the
> other thing about evolution is that anything
> can be said because very little can be dis-
> proved. Experimental evidence is minimal.[5]

I will now provide an example of the claim that evolutionary theory can be used to explain anything and everything. This is taken from Francisco Ayala, a biologist and
ardent anti-creationist,[6]

> Two criticisms of the theory of natural selec-
> tion have been raised by philosophers of sci-
> ence. One criticism is that the theory of nat-
> ural selection involves circularity. The other
> is that it cannot be subjected to an empirical
> test.

5. *New Scientist,* 166:45, 2000
6. *The Role of Natural Selection in Human Evolution*, F. M. Salzano, Ed., North Hol-
land Publ. Co., 1975, p. 19

Again, we need to be reminded that any theory that cannot be subjected to empirical test cannot qualify as a scientific theory. Ayala, of course, does not agree with those philosophers of science who challenge the scientific status of evolutionary theory, but he, as we shall see shortly, unwittingly revealed the fact that evolutionary theory, because it is so constructed that it explains everything and anything, no matter what the data are, does not qualify as a scientific theory.

In his chapter, "Scientific Hypotheses, Natural Selection and the Neutrality Theory of Protein Evolution," Ayala got off to a good start when he correctly pointed out that:

> A hypothesis or theory compatible with all possible states of affairs in the world of experience is uninformative....The important point is that the empirical content of a hypothesis is measured by the class of its potential falsifiers.

What he is saying here is that a theory that is stated in such broad or vague terms that there is no way to show that it is wrong (if it is wrong) is a very poor theory; at the very least it is not a scientific theory. A theory, to qualify as a scientific theory, must make definite predictions, the failure of which would falsify the theory. Any theory that is thus so plastic that all possible results, no matter what they may be, can be accommodated within its general concepts is not a scientific theory.

Now let us see what Ayala has to say on the very next page of his article. Perhaps he has a very short memory, or perhaps a considerable time span elapsed between the time he wrote the material on the first page and the material on the second page. On the next page of his chapter, Ayala states

> Natural selection can account for the different patterns, rates, and outcomes of evolutionary processes. Adaptive radiations in some cases, as well as lack of phyletic diversifications in others, rapid and slow rates in evolutionary change, profuse and limited genetic variation in populations; these and many other alternative occurrences can all be explained by postulating the existence of appropriate environmental challenges.

Thus, it makes no difference what the data turn out to be, one can imagine an evolutionary scenario to account for the data. Thus, the theory of natural selection can be used to explain anything and everything:

1. *Adaptive radiations* which produce numerous and widely diverse evolutionary products; or *little or no adaptive radiations*, producing practically no phyletic diversification.
2. *Rapid rates* in evolutionary change or *slow rates* in evolutionary change
3. *Profuse* genetic variations, or *limited* genetic variations
4. Many other alternative occurrences by postulating the existence of appropriate environmental challenges.

In other words, the "explanatory" power of natural selection in evolutionary theory to account for what we see in the fossil record and among living creatures today is limited only by the powers of human imagination. Thus, Ayala's cherished theory of natural selection, the driving and guiding force in evolution according to Ayala and textbook orthodoxy, is compatible with all possible states of affairs in the world of experience and therefore, according to Ayala himself, is uninformative. Furthermore, the empirical content of the theory is practically non-existent because its class of potential falsifiers is empty.

It is clear that evolution is non-falsifiable. This has been explicitly stated by numerous evolutionists.[7] Any theory that is non-falsifiable is not a scientific theory, and this applies equally to creation and evolution.

But, nevertheless, you will argue that the present paradigm, Darwinian evolution, has been so abundantly verified, that it is foolish to attempt to deny the fact of evolution. We see that expressed incessantly in evolutionary literature. Recently, however, not only creation scientists but increasing numbers of evolutionists are voicing serious doubts concerning its validity. Gareth Nelson and Norman Platnick state that,

> We believe Darwinism has an identity within
> the area of biological systematics, that it has
> a history within that discipline, that it is, in

---

7. for several examples consult my book *Creation Scientists Answer Their Critics*, pp. 35-36

short, a theory that has been put to the test and found false.[8]

An evolutionist reviewing a recent book by another (but more critical) evolutionist, says:

> We cannot identify ancestors or "missing links," and we cannot devise testable theories to explain how particular episodes of evolution came about. Gee is adamant that all the popular stories about how the first amphibians conquered the dry land, how the birds developed wings and feathers for flying, how the dinosaurs went extinct, and how humans evolved from apes are just products of our imagination, driven by prejudices and preconceptions.[9]

Marjorie Grene, the well-known philosopher and historian of science, then a professor at the University of California, Davis, also expressed her dissent. She stated that,

---

8. *Beyond Neo-Darwinism*, Chapter 6, "Systematics and Evolution," Academic Press, 1984, p. 143
9. Peter Bowler, *American Scientist*, 88:169, 2000, in his review of a book by Henry Gee

There are, indeed, all the minute specialized divergences like those of the Galapagos finches which so fascinated Darwin; it is their story that is told in the *Origin* and elaborated by the selectionists today. But these are dead ends, last minutiae of development; it is not from them that the great massive novelties of evolution could have sprung...That the color of moths and snails or the bloom on the caster bean stem are "explained" by mutation and natural selection is very likely; but how from single-celled (or for that matter from inanimate) ancestors there came to be castor beans and moths and snails, and how from these there emerged llamas and hedgehogs and lions and apès—and men— that is a question which neo-Darwinian theory simply leaves unasked.[10]

Biochemist James Shapiro at the University of Chicago said:

---

10. *Encounter*, Nov. 1959, p. 54

There are no detailed Darwinian accounts
for the evolution of any fundamental bio-
chemical or cellular system, only a variety
of wishful speculations.[11]

An evolutionary author by the name of Takahata,
recently writing about molecular anthropology, stated:

Even with DNA sequence data, we have
no direct access to the processes of evolution, so objective reconstruction of the van-
ished past can be achieved only by creative
imagination.[12]

"Wishful speculations?" "Creative imagination?" These
are hardly phrases one would expect to hear when dealing
with an idea that is supposedly equal with observable, test-
able science!

The following remarks are taken from Michael Behe's
Darwin's Black Box,[13]

---

11. *The New York Times*, Oct. 29, 1996 p. 15
12. *Annual Review of Ecology and Systematics* 26:343-72
13. the Free Press, 1996, p. 26

Lynn Margulis is Distinguished University Professor of Biology at the University of Massachusetts. Lynn Margulis is highly respected for her widely accepted theory that mitochondria, the energy source of plant and animal cells, were once independent bacterial cells. And Lynn Margulis says that history will ultimately judge neo-Darwinism as a minor twentieth-century religious sect within the sprawling religious persuasion of Anglo-Saxon biology. At one of her many public talks she asks the molecular biologists in the audience to name a single, unambiguous example of the formation of a new species by the accumulation of mutations. Her challenge goes unmet. Proponents of the standard theory, she says, "wallow in their zoological, capitalistic, competitive, cost-benefit interpretation of Darwin—having mistaken him...Neo-Darwinism, which insists on the slow accrual of mutations, is a complete funk."

The late Colin Patterson, senior paleontologist at the British Museum of Natural History, stated that,

> As it turns out, all one can learn about the history of life is learned from systematics, from the groupings one finds in nature. The rest of it is story telling of one sort or another. We have access to the tips of the tree; the tree itself is theory, and people who pretend to know about the tree and to describe what went on it—how the branches came off and the twigs came off—are, I think, telling stories.[14]

I found the following Letter to the Editor in *Geotimes*,[15]

> Chuck Berkstresser in his January 2005 letter laments that the teaching of macroevolution (evolution) has experienced a setback in the last two decades because the creationists and intelligent designers have pretty much

---

14. As quoted by Brian Leith, in an interview on BBC Radio, *The Listener* 106:390 1981
15. April 2005, p. 6.

won the hearts and minds of the public. He wonders how evolutionists can convince the public that "scientific theories are determined in a manner different and more rationally than other theories."

I've heard this same complaint from physicists and chemists leveled at the evolutionists. Evolutionists have "Physics Envy." They tell the public that the science behind evolution is the same science that sent people to the moon and cures diseases. It's not.

The science behind evolution is not empirical, but forensic. Because evolution took place in history, its scientific investigations are after the fact—no observations, no testing, no repeatability, no falsification, nothing at all like physics. They are like the people on *CSI*, only the crime scene is much older.

I think this is what the public discerns—that evolution is just a bunch of just-so stories disguised as legitimate science.

John Chaikowsky, Godfrey, ILL

John Campbell declared that:

> One can account for the sway of neo-Darwinism over the evolutionary community only by the charisma of the mathematical statement. Every one of its underlying biological tenets has proven to be a misconception...The disparities between neo-Darwinism and reality are so overwhelming that current biologists are scrambling for a completely fresh conceptual framework for the evolutionary process.[16]

Kenneth Hsu, chairman of earth sciences at the Swiss Federal Institute of Technology, says that:

> We were victims of a cruel social ideology that assumes that competition among individuals, classes, nations or races is the natural condition of life, and that it is also natural for the superior to dispossess the inferior... The law of natural selection is not, I will

---

16. *In Entropy, Information, and Evolution*, B. Weber, et al., eds. MIT Press, 1988, p. 276

maintain, science. It is an ideology, and a wicked one...[17]

How much do we know about evolution, which evolutionists declare is a proven fact? John Endler and Tracy McLellan tell us that:

> A large number of processes cause and direct evolution, but we know virtually nothing about most of them...We know virtually nothing about the complex interactions within organisms or between organisms and their environment, and how this biases or constrains the rates and directions of evolution.[18]

Finally, I wish to call your attention to a book published by the well-known evolutionary Swedish biologist, Søren Løvtrup. In his book Løvtrup reviews the development of Darwin's theory from his early work until the formulation of the present neo-Darwinian theory. He tells us why he cannot accept its central concepts of mutation and natural

17. *Earthwatch*, March 1989, p. 17
18. *American Rev. Ecol. Syst.* 1988. 19:395—421

selection. He then describes his own ideas of evolution, which embody the notion that evolution has occurred by large jumps, something similar to Goldschmidt's "hopeful monster" idea. In one of his closing statements Løvtrup declares:

I believe that one day the Darwinian myth will be ranked the greatest deceit in the history of science.[19]

Now that is an astounding statement! What Løvtrup declares to be the greatest deceit in the history of science is being taught as proven fact, not to be doubted or challenged in any way, in most of our schools and practically all of our universities. Darwinism is chiseled in stone. I have had almost 300 debates with evolutionists, and everyone, without exception, as far as I can recall, accepted the neo-Darwinian theory. Of course, we creation scientists agree with Løvtrup. We go further and declare that evolution itself is the greatest deceit in the history of science. Not that evolutionists are deliberately deceitful or dishonest, but they have been deceived or have deceived themselves in

---

19. *Darwinism:The Refutation of a Myth*, 1987, p. 422

believing what constitutes the greatest deceit in the history of science.

Evolutionists control our educational system. If a student wishes to get a doctorate in a natural science in a public university in the United States, and it becomes known that he is a creationist, he will not be allowed to work for a Ph.D. in virtually any of these schools, no matter how brilliant his academic record. A few will allow him to obtain a masters degree. Kurt Wise did get his Ph.D. under Stephen Gould at Harvard but Gould had no idea Wise was a creationist when he accepted him. I was told that he was quite angry when he found out but he recognized that Wise was a brilliant student. Evolutionists control our scientific journals. Evolutionists point out that creation scientists don't publish in standard scientific journals. Of course not! To be published in one of these journals an article must be accepted by the editor and three referees. If there is even a slight hint in the article that questions evolution or (oh my!) that it gives a tiny hint that the data suggest creation, it is summarily rejected. Even the Nobel Prize winner in physics, Hannes Alfven, complained that it was now extremely difficult for him to get his articles published.[20] His sin? He no longer supported the Big Bang theory for the origin of

20. *American Scientist May/June,* 1988, p. 249

the universe, but was suggesting a plasma theory for its origin. Sacred dogma must not be challenged or your career and your status will suffer; and sometimes even your sanity may be called into question.

Evolutionists insist that, no matter what the evidence may indicate, the concept of creation as an explanation for origins must be excluded because it is not science. They insist that evolution theory is science. Thus, by definition, evolution wins and evidence for creation, no matter how persuasive, is summarily dismissed. I remember attending a debate in which the evolutionist (I believe it was William V. Mayr) declared that even if God created DNA we can't teach that because it isn't science. A similar view was voiced by a professor in the Department of Biology at Kansas State University who said "Even if all the data point to an intelligent designer such a hypothesis is excluded from science because it is not naturalistic."[21] Earlier, however, I have documented that neither evolution nor creation are scientific theories. As Richard Lewontin, an evolutionist biologist at Harvard, has declared, creation and evolution are irreconcilable worldviews. A worldview is basically metaphysical, solidly entrenched in religious convictions.

---

21. Scott C. Todd, "A View from Kansas on the Evolution Debates," *Nature* 401: 423, 1999

The American Humanist Society has stated that humanism is a non-theistic religion. The basic fundamental dogma of humanism is evolution. Evolution is no more scientific than creation and it is just as religious.

The Random House College Dictionary defines religion as "a set of beliefs concerning the cause, nature, and purpose of the universe."[22] Certainly, evolution is used by evolutionists to do all of those things (the universe has no purpose). In a book co-authored by Julian Huxley and Jacob Bronowski we find the following dedication of evolution to religion:

> A religion is essentially an attitude to the world as a whole. Thus evolution, for example, may prove as powerful a principle to coordinate man's beliefs and hopes as God was in the past.[23]

This is about as much a religious statement that any could be. Marjorie Greene put it this way:

22. Revised Edition, 1982, p. 1114
23. *Growth of Ideas*, Prentice Hall, Inc. Englewood Cliffs, N.J. 1968, p. 99

It is as a religion of science that Darwinism chiefly held, and holds men's minds...The modified, but still characteristically Darwinian theory has itself become an orthodoxy, preached by its adherents with religious fervor and doubted, they feel, only by a few muddlers imperfect in scientific faith.[24]

Dr. Michael Ruse, a philosopher of science, was one of the chief witnesses, if not the chief witness, for the evolutionist side, at the creation/evolution trial in Federal Court at Little Rock, Arkansas, in 1981 (as you know, the judge declared the law, passed by a large majority in the Arkansas legislature that required the evidence for both creation and evolution to be taught in public schools, to be unconstitutional). When on the stand, Ruse declared that evolution was science and creation was religion. Nearly twenty years later, May 13, 2000, he published an article in the *National Post*, a Canadian newspaper. In the article he reported that during the trial I had challenged him in a personal conversation (I was only one of those in the audience with no part in the trial) that evolution was just as religious as creation. He said he pooh-poohed that idea at the time but going home

24. *Encounter,* Nov. 1959, p. 49

on the airplane while thinking about it, he began to realize that there may be some truth to this. He then describes the results of his research on this subject during the past 20 years. Although still a Darwinian evolutionist, he declared that he now believes that "Evolution is promoted by its practitioners as more than mere science. **Evolution is promulgated as an *ideology*, a secular religion—a full-fledged alternative to Christianity, with meaning and morality...*Evolution* is a religion,"** p. B1 (emphasis added). If this is true (and it surely is), then why must the evidence for evolution be taught in the public schools of our pluralistic democratic society with the exclusion of the scientific evidence for creation? Today, non-theistic evolutionary humanism is the unofficial state-sanctioned religion in our tax-supported public schools, in violation of the separation of church and state, which is supposedly required by the U.S. Constitution.

You say you believe that you can separate methodological naturalism (science) from metaphysical naturalism (religion). You cannot do that, nor can anyone else. If you accept the theory of evolution as the way the universe and living things came into being, you cannot invoke God in any way, not even in the slightest way, in evolution. **Your**

theory of evolution must be absolutely naturalistic with the total exclusion of God, or you have no theory of evolution. Darwin realized this, for he declared that if God had to be involved, his theory was absolutely worthless. If you insist that God was involved in some way, that He really is our Creator, please describe something that God had to do or else the universe and living things could not have come into existence. Of course if you can, *then you have no theory of evolution.* You cannot invoke any supernatural act of God in the evolutionary process. This is the very reason evolutionists insist that, no matter what the evidence may suggest, the possibility of supernatural creation is excluded. Since God could not have been involved, there can be absolutely no evidence for creation they say. No Creator, no evidence for creation. End of discussion. Regardless of anybody's personal faith or belief, evolution is being taught in most of our schools and universities as a strictly non-theistic, naturalistic theory. Dr. Godfrey, regardless of your personal faith, you are teaching the students that come to your church, by your commitment to methodological naturalism as applied to your theory of evolution, exactly the same theory about origins that they are being taught at the university. The difference is you believe in God and most of the professors do not.

Now I want to present evidence that is not only contradictory to, but is incompatible with evolutionary theory. If these facts are true, evolution cannot be true. As you must be aware, there occurred what is often called the "Cambrian Explosion." I do not find any discussion, however, of this paleontological dilemma in your book. Scattered around the world are what are called Cambrian rocks, identified by the presence of fossil trilobites and certain fossils of brachiopods. The Cambrian deposits are said to constitute the Cambrian Period. About 40 years ago or so, the beginning of the Cambrian Period was said to have occurred six hundred million years ago and to have been laid down during 80 million years. Now, the beginning is said to have occurred about 530 million years ago and to have required even as little as five million years to form. Dating methods do seem to be rather plastic. This reminds me of an article about the dating of "Lucy," I believe it was. The title was "The Problem of Dating an Older Woman." In the Cambrian deposits are billions times billions of fossils of complex invertebrates—trilobites, brachiopods, clams, snails, sponges, jellyfish, sea lilies, and many others. Evolutionists believe, of course, that these creatures evolved, beginning with microscopic organisms, and that they had diversified from common ancestors. Generally lying underneath the Cambrian rocks are what are called Precambrian rocks. Evolutionists believe these rocks formed during hundreds of millions of years preceding and leading up to the Cambrian. Assuming that all of this is true, what **must be found** in Precambrian rocks? In the Precambrian deposits we must find billions times billions of the fossils of the creatures intermediate between microscopic creatures and the complex invertebrates. Furthermore, we must find the transitional forms indicating that the Cambrian invertebrates arose from a common ancestor, or ancestors. The Cambrian invertebrates are so basically different from one another, they are placed in separate phyla. What do we find in the Precambrian? **Nowhere on the face of the earth have fossilized ancestors to a single one of the Cambrian invertebrates been found!** Furthermore, there are no transitional forms linking the Cambrian invertebrates to common ancestors. This is so widely acknowledged by paleontologists that I really do not need to supply documentation, but I will do so nonetheless. Douglas Futuyma states that,

It is considered likely that all the animal phyla became distinct before or during the Cambrian, for they all appear fully formed without intermediates connecting one phylum to another.[25]

Richard Dawkins has said that

...the Cambrian strata of rocks, vintage about 600 million years, are the oldest in which we find most of the major invertebrate groups. And we find many of them already in an advanced state of evolution, the very first time they appear. It is as though they were just planted there, without any evolutionary history. Needless to say, this sudden appearance of sudden planting has delighted creationists.[26]

25. Douglas Futuyma, *Evolutionary Biology* 2nd Ed., 1986, p. 325
26. *The Blind Watchmaker,* 1987, p. 229

Thomas Hayden says that

> New research shows that evolution works
> in ways that Darwin did not imagine. Many
> creatures still appear quite suddenly in the
> fossil record, and the growing suspicion
> is that evolution sometimes leaps, rather
> than crawls. For example, the first com-
> plex animals, including worms, mollusks,
> and shrimp-like arthropods, show up 545
> millions years ago; paleontologists have
> searched far and wide for fossil evidence
> of gradual progress towards these advanced
> creatures but have come up empty. "Paleon-
> tologists have the best eyes in the world,"
> says Whitey Hagadorn of Amherst College,
> who has scoured the rocks of the Southwest
> and California for signs of the earliest ani-
> mal life. "If we can't find the fossils, some-
> times you have to think that they just aren't
> there."

I have studied extensively the paleontological literature and I can attest to the fact that no one has even approached a solution concerning what George Gaylord Simpson calls "the major mystery of the history of life."[27] In my book, *Evolution: The Fossils Still Say No*, I record descriptions by evolutionists of this mystery (pp 53-69). By the way, I intend to revise and update that book this year, and someone has suggested that I title it *Evolution: The Old Fossil Still Says No!* I am seriously considering that suggestion.

This discontinuity is so complete and so extensive that this evidence alone is sufficient to disprove evolution. It is just not possible for an evolutionary process, supposedly extending over hundreds of millions of years during which time a microscopic organism gives rise to this great array of complex invertebrates, and **not leave a trace**. The Precambrian rocks should have billions times billions of the fossilized intermediate stages between the single-celled ancestor and these complex invertebrates. Our museums should have an abundance of these fossils. According to evolutionary theory, the fittest organisms are those that reproduce in larger numbers than the ones that are replaced. Each intermediate stage would thus exist in huge numbers and would persist for millions of years, giving adequate

27. *The Meaning of Evolution*, Yale U. Press, 1949, p. 18

time for extensive fossilization of each of these stages. There are many reports in the paleontological literature of the discovery of fossils of single-celled soft-bodied microscopic bacteria and algae in Precambrian rocks. If we can find fossils of microscopic organisms, we should certainly have no trouble finding fossils of intermediates between these creatures and the complex invertebrates. What greater proof for creation could we have than this tremendous discontinuity? Evolution requires continuity and here it fails absolutely.

Some trilobites have eyes with perfect undistorted vision, as perfect as any eyes in existence today. There are more than 600 lens in each eye. These lens still exist today because they are composed of inorganic crystalline calcium carbonate. Scientists were thus able to study the optics of these eyes and were astounded at what they discovered. The trilobite employed Fermat's principle, Abbe's sine law, Snell's law of refraction, and the optics of birefringent crystals to construct each lens. Dr. Godfrey, do you really believe that the ancestors of the trilobite, via random genetic errors, with no plan or purpose and with no goal in mind (there is no mind), could invent and utilize Fermat's principle, Abbe's sine law, Snell's law of refraction and the optics of birefringent crystals to construct lens with perfect undistorted vision? They had to discover something else by chance. Undistorted vision under water requires that each lens must be a double lens, and each lens of the trilobite is double. Furthermore, we don't "see" with our eyes (they are required, of course). We "see" with our brain. During the time the trilobite eye was evolving, the millions of optic nerves that carry electrical impulses to the brain would have had to evolve, and the brain would have had to evolve and somehow make the right connections between the nerves and the brain cells in order for the brain to create an image. To believe that evolution could accomplish this requires an incredible blind faith while excluding credible evidence for an intelligent agent.

There are fossils of creatures found in what is considered to be Precambrian, or nearly so. In addition to fossils of microscopic organisms, the Ediacaran Fauna, found in Australia, Newfoundland, England, Siberia, and South Africa, is said to be Precambrian. Earlier it was believed that the fossils found there may possibly resemble such things as jellyfish, sea pens, and worms, and other coelenterates and echinoderms. Now, however, it is recognized that they are so basically different from Cambrian creatures that they could not possibly be ancestral to these creatures and it is believed that they were eliminated by a mass extinction prior to the origin of the Cambrian.[28]

A recent discovery throws a monkey wrench in evolutionary thinking. It has always been assumed, totally void of any evidence, as I will document, that one or more of the Cambrian creatures gave rise to fish. This, of course, occurred subsequent to the Cambrian, and this accounts, it is said, for the lack of evidence for fossil fish in Cambrian rocks. Some earlier finds had possibly cast doubts on this assumption, but now we have solid proof. The discovery of about **500 fossil specimens of an agnathan fish in Early (Lower) Cambrian rocks** near Kunning, Yunnan, China, was reported by D. G. Shu, et al.[29] Now, by evolutionary assumptions, **these fish must have been in existence at the same time as the complex invertebrates that existed in Lower Cambrian times.** If they evolved from one or more of these invertebrates why are they found coexisting with those creatures? Paleontologists have been searching those rocks for about 200 years. Why haven't they found fossils of those fish in Lower Cambrian rocks long before now? It appears that evolutionists will have to appeal to

28. S.J. Gould, Natural History 93(2): 14-23; J. S. Levinton, *Scientific American* 267:86, 1992; J. W. Valentine, *Paleobiology* 16(1): 94, 1990
29. *Nature* 421:526-529 (2003)

the same idea that creation scientists have used to explain why they believed we hadn't found vertebrates in Cambrian deposits—there existed a significant difference in the ecological distribution of fish and these bottom dwelling creatures. Thus, because they were suddenly and catastrophically buried, fossil fish would be found in deposits above those occupied by most invertebrates. Dr. Godfrey, how do you account for the discovery of fish in Lower Cambrian Rocks?

There is another discontinuity in the paleontological record that is so immense and so complete that it is incompatible with evolutionary theory. This is the total lack of any fossils of creatures intermediate between invertebrates and fish. As mentioned earlier, there are billions times billions (and probably times billions again) of fossils of complex invertebrates. There are also billions times billions of fossil fish. If evolution is true, we should have little trouble finding fossils of the intermediate stages between invertebrates and fish. In fact, billions times billions of fossils of these intermediates must exist. Again, our museums should have an abundance of these fossils, revealing most of the intermediate stages between the invertebrate ancestor or ancestors and each of the major kinds of fish. Just the opposite is true. Each major kind of fish appears fully formed with no intermediates linking them to an invertebrate ancestor or to one of the other major kinds of fish. A.N. Strahler, in his anti-creationist book, *Science and Earth History*,[30] very well documents that fact. His book includes a review of two of my books on the fossil record.[31] This is what he has to say concerning ancestors and transitional forms for fish:

> Duane Gish finds from reading Alfred S. Romer's 1966 treatise, *Vertebrate Paleontology*, that mainstream paleontologists have found no fossil record of transitional chordates leading up to the appearance of the first class of fishes, the Agnatha, or of transitional forms between the primitive, jawless agnaths and the jaw-bearing class Placodermi, or of transition from the placoderms (which were poorly structured for swimming) to the class Chondrichthyes, or from those cartilaginous-skeleton shark-like fishes to the class Osteicthyes, or bony

30. Prometheus Book, 1987, p. 316
31. *Evolution: The Fossils Say No*, 1978; *Evolution: The Challenge of the Fossil Record,* 1985

fishes to the class Osteicthyes, or bony fishes.[32] The evolution of these classes is shown in Figure 43.1. Neither, says Gish, is there any record of transitional forms leading to the rise of the lungfishes and the crossopterygians from the lobe-finned bony fishes, an evolutionary step that is supposed to have led to the rise of amphibians and ultimately to the conquest of the lands by air-breathing vertebrates.

In a series of quotations from Romer (1966), Gish finds all the confessions he needs from the evolutionists that each of these classes appears suddenly and with no trace of ancestors. The absence of the transitional fossils in the gaps between each group of fishes and its ancestor is repeated in standard treatises on vertebrate evolution. Even Chris McGowan's 1984 anticreationist work, purporting to show "why the creationists are wrong," makes no mention of Gish's four pages of text on the origin of the fish classes. Knowing that McGowan is an authority on vertebrate paleontology, keen on faulting

32. 1978a, pp. 66-70; 1985, pp. 65-69

the creationists at every opportunity, I must assume that I haven't missed anything important in this area. This is one count in the creationists' charge that can only invoke in unison from the paleontologists a plea of *nolo contendere*

Now please note, Dr. Godfrey, you and other evolutionists have **no defense** in this case. You must simply plead *nolo contendere* or "no defense." Every one of the major kinds of fish (each class) appears **fully formed**. There are **no traces** of fossilized transitional forms linking invertebrates to fish and there are **no traces** of transitional forms linking each major kind of fish to any other kind of fish. As is the case with the complex invertebrates, every indication is that they were planted there with no evolutionary history. Again, you cannot have millions of years of evolution during which some invertebrate or invertebrates evolved into a fish, which then evolved into a variety of other fish **without leaving a trace. That is simply impossible**. As Errol White said years ago in his presidential address to the Linnean Society of London, "But whatever ideas authorities may have on the subject, the lungfishes, like every other group of fishes I know, have their origins firmly based in nothing..."[33] Later he went on to say, "I have often thought how little I should like to prove organic evolution in a court of law."

As far as common sense seems to indicate, based on these major features of the fossil record, the question of creation versus evolution is settled—**there is no question that evolution has not taken place on this planet.** It is futile for evolutionists to claim, as they often do, that they have "truck loads of transitional forms." First of all, they don't. Stephen Jay Gould has stated that:

> The extreme rarity of transitional forms in the fossil record persists as the trade secret of paleontology. The evolutionary trees that adorn our textbooks have data only at the tips and nodes of their branches; the rest is inference, however, reasonable, not the evidence of fossils.[34]

Creation scientists go further and declare that there are **no** transitional forms between the major kinds of plants or

33. Proc. Linn. Soc., London, 177:8, 1966
34. S. J. Gould, *Natural History*, 86(5): 13 (1977)

animals. Colin Patterson, with the great collection of fossils available at the British Museum of Natural History, in reply to the question why he had not illustrated any examples of transitional forms in his book, *Evolution*, 1978, replied, "I fully agree with your comments on the lack of direct illustrations of evolutionary transitions in my book. If I knew of any, living or fossil, I would certainly have included them."[35] Every one of the alleged examples of transitional forms cited by evolutionists is questionable and open to dispute. Such classical cases as the australopithecines (Johanson's "Lucy," for example,), *Archaeopteryx, Mesonyx, Basilosaurus*, the coelacanth-*Latimeria,* and *Homo habilis*, easily come to mind.

Evolutionists claim that one of the best cases they have for evolution is the evolution of the mammal-like reptiles. The actual record does not support this notion. T. S. Kemp, in his book, *Mammal-like Reptiles and the Origin of Mammals,*[36] tells us that:

> Of course there are many gaps in the synapsid fossil record, with intermediate forms between the various known groups almost invariably unknown. p.3

35. personal communication to Luther Sunderland, April 10, 1979
36. Academic Press, 1982

The apparent rate of morphological change in the main lineages of the mammal-like reptiles varies. The sudden appearance of new higher taxa, families and even orders, immediately after a mass extinction, with all the features more or less developed, implies a very rapid evolution. p. 327

Gaps at a lower taxonomic level, species and genera, are practically universal in the fossil record of the mammal-like reptiles. In no single adequately documented case is it possible to trace a transition, species by species, from one genus to another. p. 319.

George Gaylord Simpson, in the section titled "Major Discontinuities of Record," says that:

Each one of the thirty-two orders of mammals already have their basic ordinal characteristics when they first appear, that in most cases the break is so sharp and the gap so large that the origin of the order is speculative and much disputed.[37]

---

37. *Tempo and Mode in Evolution,* 1944, p.105

In his book, *The Meaning of Evolution,*[38] Simpson, with reference to the disputes among evolutionists about the origin of new phyla, classes, and other major groups, says that **"There is in this respect a tendency toward systematic deficiency in the record of the history of life. It is thus possible to claim that such transitions are not recorded because they did not exist**, that the changes were not by transition, but by sudden leaps in evolution." This is exactly what the much maligned Richard Goldschmidt believed. No transitional forms.

It is pointless to spend time taking one side or the other in these disputes within the evolutionary camp. **Let us return to where there are no disputes, no questions, no doubts about the actual evidence—the total absence of ancestors and transitional forms for the complex invertebrates and for each class of fish. The gaps are so immense and so complete that there is no doubt that these creatures all appeared fully-formed, with no ancestors. These facts completely demolish Darwinian evolution.**

As I pointed out earlier, it is not possible, if one intends to devise a naturalistic, mechanistic theory of evolution that

---

38. 1949, p. 231

is subject to test as a scientific theory, to admit that God had anything whatsoever to do with origins. Thus, evolutionists insist that the only admissible explanation for origins is a totally atheistic theory. To suggest that the evidence supports the possibility of the intervention of an intelligent agent must be absolutely excluded. Students must be, and are being, taught atheistic evolution. Futuyma states that:

> By coupling undirected, purposeless variation to the blind, uncaring process of natural selection, Darwin made theological or spiritual explanations of the life processes superfluous. Together with Marx's materialistic theory of history and society and Freud's attribution of human behavior to influences over which we have little control, Darwin's theory of evolution was a crucial plank in the platform of mechanism...[39]

Richard Dawkins tells us that,

> Biology is the study of things that give the appearance of having been designed for a

---

39. *Evolutionary Biology*, 2nd Ed., 1986, p. 2

purpose...All appearances to the contrary, the only watchmaker in nature is the blind forces of physics, albeit deployed in a very special way. A true watchmaker has foresight; he designs his cogs and springs, and plans their interconnections, with a future purpose in his mind's eye. Natural selection, the blind, unconscious, automatic process which Darwin discovered, and which we now know is the explanation for the existence and apparently purposeful form of all life, has no purpose in mind. It has no mind and no mind's eye. It does not plan for the future. It has no vision, no foresight, no sight at all. If it can be said to play the role of watchmaker in nature, it is the *blind* watchmaker.[40]

Of course, Darwin did not "discover" any such thing (although as Colin Patterson observed, he is almost treated as deity by many evolutionists). Yes, indeed as Dawkins says, biology is the study of things that give the appearance of having been designed for a purpose. In every other

40. *The Blind Watchmaker*, 1987, pp 1,5.

example in the physical world where we identify an object that has purpose and that was designed to fulfill that purpose, we immediately recognize the fact that it had an intelligent designer. But this cannot apply in biology, according to Dawkins—his atheism must exclude what otherwise seems so obvious to the majority of thinking people. He doesn't tell us where the "blind" forces of physics, which are absolutely essential for the existence of life and the universe, came from, and he does not tell us how they happen to be deployed in a very special way—we just must assume all of this on faith. In this same book, Dawkins states (p. XII, Preface) that:

> We are entirely accustomed to the idea that complex elegance is an indicator of premeditated, crafted design. This is probably the most powerful reason for the belief, held by the vast majority of people that have ever lived, in some kind of supernatural deity. It took a very large leap of imagination for Darwin and Wallace to see that, contrary to all intuition, there is another way and, once you have understood it, a far more plausible

way, for complex "design" to arise out of simplicity. A leap of imagination so large that, to this day, many people seem still unwilling to make it.

Here we are told that Darwin's discovery involved a leap of the imagination so very large that many people are unwilling to make it. Let us examine a few of the great leaps of imagination that evolutionists are willing to make. I have earlier referred to the origin of the eye of a trilobite. What about the eyes of creatures that are supposed to be closely related? H.V. Neal and H.W. Rand state that, "The differences between the various types of annelid eyes are so great that it is impossible to believe that they are genetically related to one another."[41] This means then that evolutionists must believe either that these annelid worms are not related or they each independently evolved their eyes. Sir Stewart Duke-Elder[42] states that:

It would seem, therefore, that despite the considerable amount of thought expended on the question, the emergence of the vertebrate

---

41. Comparative Anatomy, 1943
42. Vol. 1, *System of Ophthalmology*, "The Eye in Evolution", 1958, p. 839

eye with its inverted retina of neural origin and its elaborate dioptric mechanism derived from the surface ectoderm, it is a problem as yet unsolved. Indeed, appearing as it does fully formed in the most primitive species extant today, and in the absence of transition forms with which it can be associated unless by speculative hypotheses with little factual foundation, there seems little likelihood of finding a satisfying and pragmatic solution to the puzzle presented by its evolutionary development.

John Stevens, a Ph.D. associate professor of physiology and biomedical engineering, stated:[43]

To simulate 10 milliseconds of the complete processing of even a single nerve cell from the retina would require the solution of about 500 simultaneous non-linear differential equations one hundred times and would take at least several minutes of processing time on a Cray super-computer. Keeping in

43. *Byte*, April 1985

mind that there are 10 million or more such cells interacting with each other in complex ways, it would take a minimum of a hundred years of Cray time to simulate what takes place in your eye many times every second.

In their article, "Human DNA Repair Genes," Richard Wood and coworkers describe 130 known human DNA repair genes and they say that more will be found. They state that a large proportion of DNA alterations are caused unavoidably by endogenous weak mutagens, including water, reactive oxygen species, and metabolites that can act as alkylating agents. Notice that they included water! Whether embedded in a cell or floating around in lakes, streams, or oceans, DNA would be a ready candidate for destruction even by water! They state that **"Genome instability caused by the great variety of DNA-damaging agents would be an overwhelming problem for cells and organisms if it were not for DNA repair."**[44] (Emphasis added.) These repair mechanisms are very complex. **They could not have existed independent of living cells and living cells could not have existed independent of the DNA repair mechanisms.** This is just one reason, among

---

44. *Science* 291:1284, 2001

many, why evolutionary theories on the origin of life are fairy tales.

B Cells are dependent on T Cells for activation. They have an incredible mechanism that contributes to this. There are about 10,000 proteins within B Cells that are normal to the cell. B Cells clip a nine amino acid portion from each protein and attaches it to a MHC protein. The peptide-MHC protein then moves to the surface where it becomes attached. If the B Cell has been invaded by, say, a virus, a piece of protein of nine amino acids length from the virus is also obtained and attached to a MHC protein which then moves to the membrane, where it is anchored. If a killer T Cell or a helper T Cell comes along, the cell examines the peptide-HMC complexes. If only snippets of normal protein are found, the killer T Cell moves on. If the killer T Cell detects a peptide-HMC complex from the virus, it kills the cell. If a helper T Cell detects a peptide-HMC complex from a virus or other invader, it does not kill the cell but secrets interleukin, which sets off a chain of events that sends a message to the nucleus of the cell to reproduce at a rapid rate. Eventually large amounts of antibody are extruded into the extra-cellular fluid. This is only a brief description of a small part of the incredible immunological system. My question is, how could the coupling of undirected, purposeless variation to the blind, uncaring process of natural selection (re Futuyma), or natural selection, the blind unconscious, automatic process "discovered" by Darwin (re Dawson) manage to "teach" helper and killer T Cells to recognize the one foreign peptide-MHC complex among ten thousand others that are from a normal healthy B cell? How would the B Cell "know" what to do in response to the helper T Cell? At ICR we have a book describing the human immunological system. It contains more than 700 pages and surely if we knew everything about the immunological system, the book would probably require several times 700 pages. Our immunological system is a marvelous example of intelligent design.

As you know, metamorphosis is an amazing process. In many of my debates I have challenged my evolutionary opponent to describe an evolutionary explanation for the origin of the metamorphosis of the monarch butterfly. This butterfly is an incredible creature. Those that live east of the Rocky Mountains spend the winter in Mexico. During spring and summer they migrate 3000 miles to Canada. In the fall they migrate back to Mexico, some to the same trees or rocks where their ancestors had spent the previous winter (several generations are involved in their migration to and from Canada). They thus have both an amazing memory and navigational system. Before she lays her eggs, the butterfly first tests the fluid of the milkweed (they live almost exclusively on this plant). If it does not pass the test, she moves to another plant. The life of the newly hatched monarch consists, of course, of a caterpillar. As you know, the caterpillar has legs for crawling and mouthparts for eating leaves. After growth, aided by several molts, a miraculous process begins. The caterpillar, secreting a sticky substance, attaches its tail end to a stem or other firm surface, and, assuming a J-shape, it makes one last molt, getting rid of its legs and eyes. I am told it requires less than three minutes to now change into a chrysalis, which is an incredible engineering feat in itself. Inside the chrysalis there is a little heart beating and the rest resembles green jelly. My first challenge is to ask my evolutionist opponent to describe how evolution could produce this incredible process. Remember, evolution has no goal, no purpose, no foresight, no intelligence. The changes are supposedly brought about by extremely rare "good" mutations, each of which produce only slight changes. The vast majority of mutations are bad, evolutionists tell us, but they are eliminated (all intelligent people, including evolutionists, do everything prudent to avoid mutations). My own research has convinced me that there is no such thing as a good mutation. They are all bad. Even though each change is slight, the "good" mutant has an advantage and engages in a struggle for existence with the original population, which, after many thousands of generations, is eliminated. Thus, the evolutionary process necessary to produce a chrysalis from a caterpillar would require a very large number of new genes. This would require a very long time, indeed. Of course, the intermediate stages would never survive. The chrysalis is a stage that is absolutely required for the life cycle of the butterfly, and you cannot get from the caterpillar to the chrysalis a little bit at a time. Evolution just can't work that way. In real life, we can witness the origin of the chrysalis in an amazingly short time.

Now evolution really has a hard problem. No butterfly has ever yet been produced. The blind process of evolution, with no foresight, no plan, no purpose, no intelligence, must now somehow program that jelly-like mass to produce a marvelous, beautiful butterfly, that in every detail is completely different from the caterpillar. And it must do this in a matter of only a few days! Of course, a series of extremely rare "good" mutations, each followed by a struggle for existence and elimination of the less fit, producing, a little bit at a time, an enormous number of new genes necessary to code for a butterfly, would require perhaps a million years or more. Of course, any intermediate would never survive. It would be rapidly eliminated. In the real world, after eight or nine days, or so, the adult monarch butterfly is complete. It breaks out of the chrysalis, pumps the fluid from its tummy into its wings, and after the wings dry out, the butterfly, no doubt utterly amazed to see its new existence and surroundings, flies away, and somehow knows what it must do to survive and eventually reproduce.

Not one of my evolutionary opponents has ever ventured to explain how evolution could create this marvelous process. At one of my lectures at the University of California—Davis, during the discussion following the lecture, I presented this challenge to a professor in the audience. He declined, but stated that Dr. Arthur Shapiro was in the audience and he asked him to reply. At that time, Shapiro was acting chairman of the Zoology Department. His major area of research is butterflies. I had earlier had a debate with him at a university in Northern California. During this debate he spent much time on philosophy (he required that each of us have a theologian present who supported our respective views). I had gotten better acquainted with him when I attended a lecture on butterflies he gave at San Diego State University. As I recall, he said nothing about evolution in his lecture. In my conversation with him after the lecture, he told me he was going to take a bus to just north of San Diego where he would be spending the night. I offered to drive him there, and this gave us an opportunity to get better acquainted, and we became friends, although we are at the opposite poles in our world views. Now back to Shapiro's response to the request during the lecture at Davis. He replied that previously they believed that the caterpillar had evolved before the butterfly, but now they believed it more likely that the butterfly had evolved first. Then he said, "But we have no way to explain that either." If I had put him in the audience and told him what to say, he couldn't have done a better job for me! Here was this expert whose major research was on butterflies who had to confess that he had no idea how this process could have evolved. Peter Farb said that "The term metamorphosis has been given to this miraculous change of form in most insects…There is no evidence of how such a remarkable plan of life ever came about…" [45]

---

45. *The Insects*, Life Nature Library, Time Inc., 1962, p. 56

I found the following interesting statement highlighted with large type in the *Salk Institute Signals*:[46]

> A newborn baby is a miracle of joy to its parents. It is also a miracle of biological design that starts as a single, fertilized cell and, through thousands of molecular steps, develops all the tissues, organs, and structures in exactly the right place and the proper working order to make up a new human being. How does a single cell become a complex, multilayered organism? How do cells "know" where to position a limb? Where to grow a kidney? Distinguish up from down? Back from front? Left from right?

A miracle of biological design? Yes! But evolution is supposed to just plod along with no design, no intelligence, no purpose, no goal. It is just incredible what evolution, with no guidance or help of any kind, "can do." A multitude of examples can be described that defy an evolutionary explanation. It is not that an evolutionary explanation

---

46. Vol. 3 (2) Summer 1998

has not as yet been discovered. The scientific evidence is incompatible with any notion about evolution.

Perhaps the most formidable of critics of Darwinism was St. George Mivart. Of all the objections to the theory of natural selection by Mivart, according to Stephen Jay Gould, there was one that "...stood out as the centerpiece of his criticism...It remains today the primary stumbling block among thoughtful and friendly scrutinizers of Darwinism." This was, as Mivart called it, "The incompetency of natural selection to account for the incipient stages of useful structures."

. Gould then says,

> If this phrase sounds like a mouthful, consider the easy translation: we can readily understand how complex and fully developed structures work and owe their maintenance and preservation to natural selection—a wing, an eye, the resemblance of a bittern to a branch or of an insect to a stick or dead leaf. But how do you get from nothing to such an elaborate something if evolution must proceed through a long sequence of

intermediate stages, each favored by natural selection? You can't fly with 2% of a wing or gain much protection from an iota's similarity with a potentially concealing piece of vegetation. How, in other words, can natural selection explain these incipient stages of structures that can only be used (as we now observe them) in much more elaborated form?

Gould then pointed out that among the difficulties of Darwinian theory "One point stands high above the rest: the dilemma of incipient stages. Mivart identified this problem as primary and it remains so today."[47]

Gould's solution? Perhaps in their early stages these structures served some other useful purpose. To support this "solution" one would have to postulate another theory in each case how the incipient structure performed that useful function. But then there would have been an incipient stage leading up to this useful stage. As W. R. Thompson stated in his introduction to the 1956 reprint of Darwin's *Origin of Species*,[48] evolution theory consists of hypotheses

---

47. *Natural History,* Oct. 1985, pp. 12-13
48. Everyman's Library, E. P. Dutton and Co.

piled on hypotheses where fact and fiction intermingle in an inextricable confusion.

I earlier pointed out the challenge to evolution that comes from the discovery of fish in what are called Early or Lower Cambrian deposits. Another challenge has come about recently. Evolutionists have long maintained that as long as dinosaurs existed on the earth, what mammals that existed at that time were very small. Paleontologists had succeeded in finding many fossils of dinosaurs in what is called the Mesozoic Era, but their searches had only produced fossils of tiny mammals. The explanation given was that mammals could not flourish and expand in size as long as all those dinosaurs and other creatures existed at that time. Here is the story as described by Michael D. Lemonick in *Time Magazine*[49]:

> Conventional wisdom has long held that mammals spent millions of years in Darwinian limbo. As long as dinosaurs roamed the earth, our distant ancestors never got to be much more than cringing, shrew like creatures that slinked out at night to nibble timorously on plants and insects when the

---

49. January 24, 2005, p. 56

terrible lizards were asleep. Only when a rogue comet wiped the dinosaurs out, went the story, did mammals begin to earn a little evolutionary respect.

But that picture changed dramatically last week with the announcement in *Nature* of two impressive fossils. One, of a brand-new species dubbed *Repenomamus giganticus*, demolishes the notion that most dinosaur-age mammals were never larger than squirrels. The animal, which lived some 130 million years ago, had the dimensions of a midsize dog or large badger—by far the biggest dinosaur-age mammal ever found. And the second, a new specimen of a previously discovered species called *Repenomamus robustus*, refutes the notion that it was always the mammals that got eaten. Inside the skeleton where the animal's stomach would have been are the fossilized remains of a baby dino... Taken together, the finds overturn the idea that early mammals were tiny and timid, that had been eroding anyway with occasional discoveries of teeth and bone fragments that hinted at larger creatures. Now paleontologists can stop cooking up theories to explain why mammals were so little—that they had to be small to avoid being found, for example, or they couldn't grow larger because dinosaurs already occupied those ecological niches.

Now, my question is, in all of the 175 years since dinosaurs were first discovered and during which paleontologists have been searching these rocks, why did they fail to find fossils of these large mammals? Whatever one thinks about the age of these deposits, it is now known beyond doubt that large mammals existed at the same time as these dinosaurs. Furthermore, it is virtually certain that many other kinds of large mammals existed at the same time. It seems to me evolutionists will have to postulate that mammals kept a safe distance from the dinosaurs, that they did not occupy similar habitats. What suggestion do you have to offer, Dr. Godfrey? But then, evolutionists use their theory to explain anything and everything.

Until about forty years ago, if you were a geologist and you believed in continental drift, you would have had a very difficult time getting a job or getting a promotion. Now if you are a geologist who doesn't believe in continental drift, you can't get a job or a promotion (I believe it was the British geologist, Derek Ager, a self-styled neo-catastrophist, and stanch evolutionist, who said that[50]). I wonder how it is possible for geologists to claim 50 years ago that the geological evidence proves that continents have always been right where they are now, and then later incorporate the same evidence in geological theory that postulates that continents have been drifting all over the earth, a totally different model of earth history. Furthermore, evolutionists had neat theories to explain biogeography based on fixed continents, and now they have equally neat ideas about biogeography based on continental drift.

This reminds me of the tale about Archaeoraptor, the fossil featured in the November, 1999 article, "Feathers for T. Rex?" in the *National Geographic*. Here at last was final proof, we were told, that birds had evolved from dinosaurs. The fossil appeared to have the front part of a bird and the back part of a dinosaur. It turned out to be a complete fraud— an ingenious Chinese farmer had glued the back part of a

50. *The Nature of the Stratigraphical Record*, 1973

dinosaur (or something) on the front part of a bird, greatly inflating the market value of the fossil. The exposé of this fraud brought great embarrassment to the people involved, including the scientists who participated and people at the *National Geographic Magazine*. Lewis M. Simons, a veteran investigative reporter, was commissioned by *National Geographic* to investigate all facets surrounding the fraud. Here is the introduction to his report:

> Assured of carte blanche, I traveled through parts of China and the United States, as well as up and down the halls of the Geographic in Washington; interviewed peasant farmers and Ph.D.'s, hucksters, journalists, zealots, and cranks; stared through microscopes, magnifying glasses, and into a room-size, lead-lined scanner; sent and received scores of documents, e-mails, faxes, and phone calls.
>
> Using what I've seen, heard, and read, I've assembled a brief history of *Archaeoraptor.* It's a tale of misguided secrecy and misplaced confidence, of rampant egos

clashing, self-aggrandizement, wishful thinking, naive assumptions, human error, stubbornness, manipulation, backbiting, lying, corruption, and, most of all, abysmal communication. It's a story in which none of the characters looks good.[51]

Prior to this another feathery dinosaur was deplumed. R. Monastersky tells us in *Science News*[52] that:

> If people can have their 15 minutes of fame, so can dinosaurs. Most recently, the international spotlight has focused on a chicken-size fossil from northeast China. Its body apparently fringed with downy impressions. For paleontologists who believe that birds evolved from dinosaurs, this specimen seemed the ultimate feather in their cap.
>
> An international team of researchers that examined the Chinese fossil now concludes that the fibrous structures are not feathers. Even more important for the future,

51. *National Geographic*, Oct. 2000, p. 128
52. May 3, 1997, p. 271

however, the scientists report that the fossil site is awash with specimens—some showing remarkable features seen nowhere else.

The fossil, named Sinosauropteryx, is now believed to possibly fit into the genus *Compsognathus*. The team included John Ostrom, Alan Brush, Larry Martin and Peter Wellnhofer. Larry Martin of the University of Kansas, Storrs Olson of the Smithsonian, and Alan Feduccia of the University of North Carolina, are ornithologists who believe they have found evidence that positively excludes dinosaurs as ancestors of birds. This recalls to mind the illustration of embryos published by Ernst Haeckel in 1874. This has been known to be completely fraudulent, almost as early as its publication, but research several years ago showed that it appeared in at least 50 biology texts in print at that time.[53] But, of course, it looked so convincing and so easy to teach.

In one of my debates I debated Dr. Massimo Pigliucci, a plant scientist at the University of Tennessee. He told the audience that he had produced a number of "good" mutations with his plants. I challenged his claim by asking him if he had proven this by exposing these plants to all kinds of natural conditions, such as drought, heat, cold, reduced

53. S. J. Gould, *Natural History* March 2000, pp 44-45

food, insects, natural diseases, and compare their survival rates in comparison to the original plants under the same conditions. Of course, he had done no such thing. I have a draft manuscript of a plant scientist that participated in an experiment in plant breeding, which no doubt has been published years ago, so I will not be revealing unpublished work in describing the experiment. When it was discovered that certain forms of radiation and certain chemicals were powerful mutagenic agents, many millions of plants were mutagenized and screened for improvements. Based on the assumption that random mutations would result in some improved properties, it was expected that this would result in rapid evolution. A great number of small, sterile, sick, deformed, aberrant plants were produced. Essentially, no meaningful crop improvement resulted. The entire effort was a total failure and was completely abandoned. In spite of all of these millions of mutations there were no beneficial mutations. When the plant scientists abandoned mutation breeding and instead used the pre-existing natural variation within each species or genus, they were very successful in crop improvement. Evolutionists assume that all genetic variations were produced by mutations. If this is true then obviously there must have been an enormous number of good mutations. The experience with mutations by plant scientists indicate that such is not the case. Almost every issue of the science journals have several articles identifying the deleterious effects of harmful mutations. I can't recall of ever seeing a report of a good mutation. I am convinced that all of the genes present in any plant or animal that is considered normal or healthy were present in the original created kinds. There is an incredible variation potential in each kind. For example, as Ernst Mayr has said, two people could potentially produce trillions of children without any having the exact same genetics (identical twins excepted).

In your book you claim that Genesis has two different creation accounts. However, Genesis 1 is a chronological account of creation. In Genesis 2 we have a recapitulation of creation, not to be understood as a chronological account. When I was on the research staff of the Upjohn Company in Kalamazoo, each investigator had a bound notebook in which were to be recorded and dated a description of his work each day. This was a chronological account of his research. Each year each research team gave both a written and an oral report to management. The work and accomplishments of the year were not related in a chronological order. Accomplishments that were considered the most significant may be described first and descriptions of the work that preceded and led up to the final results logically would follow. If there were any litigation involving priority in patents, the bound notebooks would be offered as evidence, not the annual reports to management.

You wish to reduce the first eleven chapters of Genesis to poetry rather than a historical narrative. That way, you believe you can read anything into it, thus you can accept what the majority of scientists, whether professing Christians, agnostics or atheistic humanists tell us about their ideas of origins. It requires some serious manipulation to read Genesis 1 to 11 as poetry. Thus, the universe was not created by God, but by a fluctuation of a false vacuum. From a point almost infinitely small, via an expansion lasting a tiny fraction of a second, there resulted something about the size of a grapefruit. This was followed by something often referred to as the Big Bang. This produced just two elements, 75% hydrogen and 25% helium, and gravity did the rest. Cosmologists must appeal to the existence of cold dark matter (can't be seen, can't be detected), and dark energy (which can't be seen and can't be detected). This energy has the remarkable property of not possessing gravity, as is true of all other matter and energy, but possesses anti-gravity. Of course, dark matter and dark energy are no more than tooth fairies that have been invented to rescue their Big Bang theory. String theory has been invented in an attempt to mitigate some other problems. This theory tells us that things like electrons don't exist at a point; but are strings almost infinitely thin. They are so thin they can't be seen, so we can't see them. On the basis of string theory, it is postulated that the universe has ten dimensions. That is also supposed to help somehow. All of this is nothing more than mental mathematics. It is certainly not observational science.

The discovery, of large numbers of mature galaxies, in an area that supposedly existed very near the beginning of the universe, and the discovery that all the lights in the universe came on at the same time in one great burst, according to a research team that included John Bahcall of the Institute for Advanced Study in Princeton, New Jersey, was recorded in an article in *Time Magazine*.[54] These discoveries were a great surprise to these astronomers. If they were truly seeing what existed at a time very early in the lifespan of the universe, they should certainly not be looking at mature, or relatively old, universes. I predict, furthermore, when astronomers are able to look out far enough to what

---

54. Nov. 3, 1997, p. 34-36.

they believe to be the universe very nearly at the beginning, they won't be seeing these gases which they assume is all that existed at that "time", but they will see stars and mature galaxies. The fact that all the lights in the universe came on at the same time, as they proclaimed, is absolutely contrary to the Big Bang Theory, or to any theory of an evolutionary origin of the universe. If evolution is true, as the first stars formed the light of each would turn on in the sequence of their origin, then the light of the first galaxy would turn on, and so on, as succeeding stars and galaxies formed. But this is not what they saw. **All the lights came on in one great burst!** This fact is incompatible with an evolutionary origin of the universe but is exactly in accord with creation as described in Genesis. The solution to their dilemma would have come quickly if they had only read Genesis 1.

There is additional irrefutable scientific evidence against the Big Bang Theory, or any similar theory, such as inflation theory coupled with a subsequent scenario similar to the Big Bang. It is almost universally acknowledged that (if there is no God, or if God would not choose to intervene), the natural universe is certain to die. Our sun is said to be burning up several tons of fuel every second. Every star in the universe is burning up its fuel. It is obvious that the day will come, if this natural process is allowed to proceed, when every star in the universe will have burned up its fuel. Then the universe will be dead—no more activity, no life. The natural laws and natural processes which now govern the universe are causing its inevitable death and destruction (if God does not intervene, but II Peter 3 declares that He will). Evolutionists declare that these natural laws and processes are all there is and all there ever has been. **How, then, could these very same natural laws and processes which are destroying the universe be responsible for its origin?** What sort of tortured logic would lead one to such an impossible conclusion?

This evidence confirms two statements found in the Bible. It confirms the literal truth of Psalm 102:26. In this verse, speaking of the heavens and the earth, we read "They shall perish, but thou shalt endure: Yea, *all of them shall wax old like a garment*; as a vesture shalt thou change them, and they shall be changed." The Bible thus records the fact, in a passage written 3,000 years ago, that the heavenly bodies and the earth (the universe) is wearing out, running down, proceeding inevitably to a state of greater randomness, precisely as the science of thermodynamics has established during the past 150 years, or so. Furthermore, this evidence establishes the fact that the universe had a beginning, as the Bible proclaims. If the universe had been here forever it would have rundown a long time ago. It hasn't rundown yet, so it hasn't been here forever. At the time the Bible was written most people believed the universe had been here forever and would continue to be here forever. They were wrong and the Bible was right.

The Second Law of Thermodynamics tells us that every isolated system, with no exceptions, inevitably runs down and decays. An isolated system is one on which no work is being performed by anything on the outside and no energy or matter enters the system from the outside. Everything that takes place within the system is a process of self-transformation. The order and complexity within such a system never increases. Evolutionists believe, contrary to this natural law, that the universe is an isolated system which began with the disorder and chaos of the Big Bang and the simplicity of hydrogen and helium gases and transformed itself into the incredible complex of the universe that exists today.

Dr. Godfrey, using your position as a methodological naturalist, and thus your assumption that the origin of all things in nature, including the universe, can be explained by the action of natural laws, please explain how the universe could have created itself. The self-creation of the universe would have required the violation of natural law. **In fact you cannot appeal to natural laws, since, according to evolutionists, there were no natural laws before the Big Bang.**

Evolutionists believe that the natural laws that govern the universe, somehow just popped into existence out of the Big Bang. Here again, they find themselves in an impossible situation. It is now known that nearly 50 physical constants must be precisely as they are for the universe and living organisms to exist. These include the universal constants (Boltzman's constant, Planck's constant, the speed of light, and gravitational constant); the mass of elementary particles (pion rest-mass/energy, neutron rest mass/energy, electron rest mass, unit charge, mass-energy relation); and fine structure constants (gravitational, weak interaction, electromagnetic, and strong interaction fine constants). If any of these constants varied slightly our universe could not exist or support life.[55] Each one of the physical constants that control our universe or are necessary for the existence of life have the exact value required. Physicists have no idea why this is so. The probability that **even one** of these

55. Paul Davies, *The Accidental Universe,* Cambridge University Press, 1982; p. III; as quoted by Wolfgang Smith, *Teilhardism and the New Religion*, Tan Books and Pub. Rockford, IL, 1988, p. 12

physical constants would have the exact value required out of an almost infinite number of values that could be produced by a theoretical Big Bang, is **essentially infinitely improbable**. One cannot even calculate the improbability that two, three, four, or five, not to mention fifty or so of these constants would accidentally be right out of an infinite number of possibilities. Richard Dawkins said that Darwin had to make a great leap of imagination in order to suggest that the notion of natural selection explained the origin of things that appeared to have been created for a purpose. To accept the idea that all of the physical constants just happened somehow to be exactly as required by chance is a leap of imagination that is infinitely unreal.

I am enclosing a copy of an article by evolutionist Eric Lerner giving arguments against the Big Bang theory.[56] The article was signed by 33 other scientists from 10 different countries. They are all evolutionists but reject the Big Bang Theory as scientifically untenable. This is what Sir Fred Hoyle had to say about the Big Bang Theory:[57]

> But the interesting quark transformations are
> almost immediately over and done with, to

56. "Bucking the Big Bang," *New Scientist*, 22 May 2004, p.20
57. *New Scientist,* 19 Nov., 1981, p. 523

be followed by a little rather simple nuclear physics, to be followed by what? By a dull-as-ditchwater expansion which degrades itself adiabatically until it is incapable of doing anything at all. The notion that galaxies form, to be followed by an active astronomical history, is an illusion. Nothing forms, the thing is as dead as a door-nail... The punch-line is that, even though outward speeds are maintained in a free explosion, internal motions are not. Internal motions die away adiabatically, and the expanding system become inert, which is exactly why the big-bang cosmologies lead to a universe that is dead-and-done-with almost from its beginning.

You apparently reject flood geology completely. I assume you believe there was some sort of a flood, perhaps a local flood? You try to make the Bible say that the waters of the flood did not really cover all the high hills. But that is what the Bible says and what was understood until efforts began to deny any real history in Genesis 1-11. The purpose of the flood is explicitly described in Genesis 6-7. You try to change the meaning of the Hebrew word translated as "earth" to mean only "land." Thus the flood was only local and the Biblical statement is not real history that declares:

> All flesh died that moved upon the earth, both of fowl, and of cattle, and of beast, and every creeping thing that creeps upon the earth, and every man, all in whose nostrils was the breath of life, of all that was in the dry land, died. And every living substance was destroyed which was upon the face of the ground, both man, and cattle, and the creeping things, and the fowl of the heaven, and they were destroyed from the earth, and Noah only remained alive, and they that were with him on the ark (Genesis 7:21-23).

Now, obviously birds could easily avoid a local flood, and why would God have Noah build an ark and load it with all those animals to escape a local flood? It would be much easier to migrate to a safe locality.

If your construction of Genesis and your rejection of a world-wide flood are true then the prophets, the disciples, and Jesus Christ were completely confused and misled. In Isaiah 54:9 we read:

> For this is like the waters of Noah to me; for as I have sworn that the waters of Noah would no longer **cover the earth,** so I have sworn that I would not be angry with you, nor rebuke you. (NKJV, emphasis added)

In Matthew we read the very words of Christ given to us by Matthew (24:37-39):

> But as the days of Noe were, shall also the coming of the Son of man be. For as in the days that were before the flood they were eating and drinking, marrying and giving in marriage, until the day that Noe entered into the ark, and knew not until the flood came, and took them all away; so shall also the coming of the Son of man be.

In Luke (17:26), Luke also directly quotes Jesus Christ as saying:

> And as it was in the days of Noe, so shall it be also in the days of the Son of man. They did eat, they drank, they married wives, they were given in marriage, until the day that Noe entered the ark, and the flood came, and destroyed them all.

Now 2000 years later, people living two millennia after these words were recorded by those disciples, are somewhat wiser than the prophets, the disciples, and Christ, Himself, and reject what they have said and reduce the record of the flood as recorded in Genesis to poetry. This should not be a surprise, however, because the Apostle Peter prophesied that this would happen. In II Peter 3:2-6 we read:

> That ye may be mindful of the words which were spoken before by the holy prophets, and of the commandment of us the apostles of the Lord and Saviour; Knowing this first, that there shall come in the last days

scoffers, walking after their own lusts, and saying, Where is the promise of his coming? For since the fathers fell asleep, all things continue as they were from the beginning of the creation. For this they willingly are ignorant of, that by the word of God the heavens were of old, and the earth standing out of the water and in the water: Whereby the world that then was, being overflowed with water, perished:

For nearly 1800 years this prophecy went unfilled, but beginning with James Hutton and later Charles Lyell and others about the beginning of the 19th Century, the record of the flood was reduced to fiction and it was declared that no such flood ever occurred by those who were willingly blind, precisely fulfilling this prophecy. Peter admonishes us to be mindful of the words spoken before by the holy prophets and of the commandment of the apostles of the Lord and Savior. Peter tells us (II Peter 1:16) that, "For we have not followed cunningly devised fables, when we made known unto you the power and coming of our Lord Jesus Christ, but were eyewitnesses of his majesty."

You make every effort to reduce the Bible to something that has moral authority but is totally unworthy as a historical account. You say p. 139, speaking of passages in the Old and New Testament, that "They all attribute to a supernatural cause (the action of God) results which, the more closely one studies them, appear more and more to have come about through a natural process." On p. 140 you say, "This chapter is the place for us to establish that the Bible, for its part, bears all the marks of having been produced through the same process as human writings that are not considered divinely inspired" How can you possibly refer to the Bible or any portion of it as the "word of God" when you reduce it to the same level as other human writings that are not divinely inspired? This is what we hear all the time—all religions are equally valid, all of them are leading us to God. Atheistic humanists deny the existence of God and many claim that they rest on the higher ground of moral authority. Your complete capitulation to evolutionism is revealed on p. 149, where you say "And while we may conclude that the most reasonable explanation of the story told in fossils is that biological diversity is the result of an uninterrupted natural process, we may still consider human beings to posses worth and dignity because they are 'created in the image of God.'"

On page 161 you say, "We see in these chapters that what is unique about humans is not the process by which they came about, but rather the purpose for which God makes them." In your book you seek to infer that when the Bible tells us that Adam (merely a term for the first evolutionary product of *Homo sapiens*?) was created from the dust of the ground, that this is a description of the same process that brought animals into existence. Nowhere in your book have I found any mention of the creation of Eve (woman). The Bible tells us that God put Adam to sleep and from a rib that He took from Adam He created woman. It is impossible to relate this to the creation of any animal, and of course no evolutionist, atheist or theist, believes it. A chest surgeon told me that when he removes a rib for some reason, he slits open the covering of the rib, called the periosteum, removes the rib and then sews up the periosteum because the rib is the only bone in the human that regenerates itself. You say that God makes new things by starting with something that already exists, and you use the example of Christ feeding the 5,000. But of course the loaves and fish did not gradually evolve into something else. The quantity was supernaturally multiplied by Christ.

You have maintained that Genesis 1-11 is not to be taken as history but is poetry. One leading Hebrew scholar is James Barr, professor of Hebrew Bible at Vanderbilt University and former regius professor of Hebrew at Oxford University in England. Although he does not believe in the historicity of Genesis 1, Dr. Barr does agree that the writer's *intent* was to narrate the actual history of primeval creation. Others also agree with him. David Watson, a British scholar and creationist, wrote to Barr in 1984 asking what he considered to be the intent of the writer of the first eleven chapters of Genesis. Barr replied:

> Probably, so far as I know, there is no professor of Hebrew or Old Testament at any world-class university who does not believe that the writer(s) of Genesis 1-11 intended to convey to their readers the ideas that (a) creation took place in a series of six days which were the same as the days of 24 hours we now experience...Or, to put it negatively, the apologetic arguments which suppose the

"days" of creation to be long eras of time, the figures of years not to be chronological, and the flood to be a merely local Mesopotamian flood, are not taken seriously by any such professors, as far as I know.

I am enclosing a copy of the ICR Impact article #377 by Steven W. Boyd, "The Biblical Hebrew Creation Account; New Numbers Tell the Story." According to his research, Genesis 1 is certainly not poetry but is a historical narrative account just as maintained by Barr and his fellow Hebrew scholars. Critics whose intent is to discredit the Bible claim that it teaches, as you do, that there is a solid dome in the heavens and that the earth is flat. Many leading scholars of the Bible deny that this is what the Bible is saying regardless of what some people believe. You have accepted practically every interpretation in the Bible that critics use to discredit it. Anyone can find apparent errors in the Bible by a superficial examination, but good scholars, by a thorough investigation of the context, many examples of usage, the best translation of the Hebrew or Greek, genre, and other comparisons, can reach a conclusion that no error is involved. One should consult books by those who accept the inerrancy of the Bible and which are written to respond to those who seek to describe errors in the Bible.

Earlier I mentioned that I was aware of one event described in the Bible that could not be accepted as observational rather than literal. This is the account of Joshua's long day (Joshua 10:12-14). It is true that as the people looked up at the sun, it appeared to them that it stood still, and their belief is that which is recorded. Now you would say that we know that the sun really did not stand still but the earth stopped rotating. But you cannot believe that either. If the earth stopped rotating, (and we know a body in motion remains in motion unless acted on by another force), the result would be world-wide chaos—huge tidal waves, structures ripped to pieces, people and all loose objects thrown about, and so forth. One must either claim that such an event never happened, or it was under the complete control of a supernatural being. Of course, the latter is outside of methodological naturalism, so must be relegated to fiction by those who take the view that God could not have been involved here anymore than in the world wide flood.

You suggest that the existence of light on the earth starting on the first day was a problem that required an explanation. The explanation is very simple. Light, which is energy, was created on the first day, and the earth in its incomplete form, could be bathed in this light. What happened to this enormous quantity of light that God created? Although restricted to speculation (as is all of cosmogony), I believed it is very likely that the universe was created by God by the conversion of this energy into matter. The sun, moon, and stars were created from this energy on the fourth day.

You say (p. 157) that there is no conceptual inconsistency between extinctions observed in the evolutionary process and biblical judgments, such as the flood. Later (p. 158) you say it would certainly not be consistent to object to the evolutionary process from a creationist perspective as unnecessarily wasteful, but then appeal to "flood geology" to explain the origin of fossils. That is completely erroneous. You believe that God used the deaths of all those animals as a means of creation. If so, just as today, enormous numbers of deaths were occurring every second, and contrary to what you claim (p. 167), death would be absolutely necessary for evolution. Natural selection would require the death of the preceding form in the struggle for existence. All leading evolutionists agree on that point.

The French geneticist Jacques Monod, whose work on the genetics of microorganisms won him a Nobel Prize, said in an interview by Laurie John, Australian Broadcasting Co., June 10, 1976,

> [Natural] selection is the blindest, and most cruel way of evolving new species... The struggle for life and elimination of the weakest is a horrible process, against which our whole modern ethics revolts...I am surprised that a Christian would defend the idea that this is the process which God more or less set up in order to have evolution.

G. Richard Bozarth, in an article in the *American Atheist*,[58] entitled "The Meaning of Evolution" said that:

> Christianity has fought, still fights, and will fight science to the desperate end over evolution, because evolution destroys utterly and finally the very reason Jesus' earthly life was supposedly made necessary. Destroy Adam and Eve and the original sin, and in

58. Feb. 1978, p. 30

the rubble you will find the sorry remains of the son of God. If Jesus was not the redeemer who died for our sins, and this is what evolution means, then Christianity is nothing.

Of course there never has been warfare between Christianity and science, although there has been and continues to be warfare between Christians and unbelieving scientists. Most of the founders of modern science—Sir Isaac Newton, James Clark Matthew, Lord Kelvin, Louis Pasteur, Robert Boyle, Michael Faraday, Carolus Linnaeus—were Christians and creationists. I think it is interesting that atheistic evolutionists, such as Monod and Bozarth, have a better insight into the real meaning of the relationship of evolution to Christianity than do many Christians.

In all of the preceding I have said little about the evolutionary origin of life. There are two reasons for this. First, this "letter" has evolved into booklet length and I am growing weary, and secondly, more and more evolutionists are giving up on solving that problem and just concede that they really do not know how life could have evolved. As a biochemist I could easily list several dozen reasons why an evolutionary origin of life on this planet would not only have been incredibly improbable, it would have been absolutely impossible. I agree with Sir Fred Hoyle who declared that the probability of an evolutionary origin of life anywhere in the universe, even if every star had a planet like the earth and the universe is 20 billion years old, would be equal to the probability that a tornado sweeping through a junkyard would assemble a Boeing 747. Sir Fred's study of the probability of an evolutionary origin of life convinced this former atheist that there had to be a God. Furthermore, concerning biological evolution, he accused evolutionists of believing in mathematical miracles.

I think I should mention that even the properties of water necessary for the existence of life are incredible. Robert Mathews, *New Scientist*,[59] presents us the following:

WHY WATER NEEDS TO BE WEIRD

We all owe our existence to the weirdness of water—as the Harvard biochemist Lawrence Henderson pointed out as long ago as 1913. For example, if water behaved like most materials and contracted on freezing rather than expanding, ice would be denser than water, and would sink to the seabed.

59. June 21, 1997, p. 43

There would be none of the insulating layers of ice that conveniently form on the surfaces of oceans and lakes, allowing marine and aquatic life to survive in the unfrozen water below. Instead, the ice would sink to the bottom, from where it would inexorably build up until the oceans froze solid.

The enormous specific heat capacity of water means that it takes a lot of solar heating to warm the oceans, and once warmed they are slow to cool. This protects us from sudden climate changes, and allows ocean currents such as the Gulf Stream to carry solar heat from the tropics towards the poles.

The anomalous behavior of water also plays a key role in life at a more fundamental level. Its relatively high surface tension leads to biological compounds concentrating near liquid surfaces, speeding up biological reactions.

The powerful solvent properties of water are also widely exploited by living creatures:

many biologically active compounds are switched on or off by changes in the concentrations of dissolved ions such as sodium and potassium. Individual water molecules, with their tendency to form hydrogen bonds, also stabiles the structure of proteins, whose action depends crucially on their shape.

It's not all good news though. That same keenness to form hydrogen bonds makes water a real headache for researchers trying to solve the mystery of the origin of life. Water tears apart the twin strands of DNA, on which life depends for reproduction. While modern forms of life have developed ways of combating this, it is hard to see how molecules such as DNA and RNA could have survived long enough on the primordial Earth to become established as the carriers of genetic information.

Tom Bethell published the following interesting comments in *Harper's Magazine*:[60]

---

60. 252:70, Feb. 1976

According to Dobzhansky, the evolutionary process is "blind, mechanical, automatic, impersonal." Sir Gavin de Beer, the British biologist and evolutionist, stated that evolution was "wasteful, blind, and blundering." When it comes to selling evolution, however, and extolling the processes involved, evolutionists wax eloquent. Dobzhansky likened natural selection to "a human activity such as performing or composing music." De Beer described it as a "master of ceremonies." Simpson compared natural selection to a poet and a builder. Ernst Mayr, formerly a professor of zoology at Harvard, likened selection to a sculptor. Sir Julian Huxley compared natural selection to William Shakespeare. To say that these evolutionists had a fondness for Darwinism bordering on obsession would hardly be an overstatement.

Dr. Godfrey, you related your change of views about the Biblical record partly to the many horizons of erect fossil trees at Joggins, Nova Scotia, Canada. I wonder how much research has been done to establish the claim they are in situ. In one of his books Ron Numbers relates that the evidence that caused him to abandon his faith was the fossil "forests" in volcanic deposits, one above the other, in and adjacent to Yellowstone National Park. For many years the Park had a plaque at a site looking towards Specimen Ridge where are found some of these trees. The text claimed that these constitute a series of fossil forests that formed successively during millions of years. Now that plaque has been removed. Geologists began studying these forests and their research led them to the hypothesis that the fossil trees did not grow where they are now, but were transported to that location together with the sediments.[61] According to Brand, several lines of research, published in professional journals, now lend support to this hypothesis.[62] I wonder what would have happened to his faith if Numbers had had this information at hand when he abandoned that faith.

I say again, Dr. Godfrey, that regardless of your personal faith, if you teach students the evolutionary paradigm, that everything began with a hypothetical Big Bang which

61. Leonard Brand, *Faith, Reason and Earth History,* Andrews University Press, Berrien Springs, MI, 1997, p. 69
62. A.V. Chadwick and T. Yamamoto, *Palaeography, Palaeoclimatology, Palaeoecology* 45:39-48 (1984); H. G. Coffin, *Journal of Paleontology* 50:539-543 (1976); Coffin, "The Puzzle of the Petrified Trees", Dialogue 4(1)11-13 (1992)

produced nothing more than hydrogen along with some helium, and employing nothing more than gravity, this gave rise to the universe, and eventually to all living things, including man, many, and most probably the majority, will conclude, "Who needs God? There is no God, and if there is no God there is no one to whom I am responsible. I am responsible only to my self." There have been enormous changes in our society in the past 60 years or more. Now we have a drug culture that is literally destroying the bodies, minds, and souls of millions of people; legalized pornography—if 60 years ago you publicly showed what you can see every night on your TV they would have put you in jail; legalized abortions that are destroying the lives of more than a million unborn children each year; churches are ordaining practicing homosexuals; mass murders are common, which were almost never heard of in the past. Of course we had immorality, crime, violence, and almost all vices in the past, but nothing on the scale now existing. I believe much of this is due to the fact that our judges, legislators, educators, and other leaders in our society have been indoctrinated in the philosophy of evolution, a non-theistic religion. With leading evolutionists, such as Richard Dawkins, (who has declared that faith is worse than small pox, only harder to eradicate), being rewarded by prestigious positions at places like Oxford University, we Christians have an uphill battle to preserve the faith once given to the saints. Dr. Godfrey, I cherish your understanding of the true nature of what we are facing in the battle to establish the truth of God's creation. "Render therefore to Caesar the things that are Caesar's, and to God the things that are God's" (Matt. 22:21; NKJV).

> Thou art worthy, O Lord, to receive glory,
> and honor, and power for thou hast created
> all things, and for thy pleasure they are and
> were created (Rev. 4:11).

Sincerely, your brother in Christ,

Duane T. Gish, PhD.
Senior Vice President Emeritus
DTG:mt
Encl.

About
the Author

Born in Kansas in 1921, Duane Gish was an Army officer in the Pacific during World War II, then returned home and earned a B.S. in chemistry from UCLA, followed by a Ph.D. in biochemistry from the University of California at Berkeley in 1953. Dr. Gish also studied at Cornell University Medical College in New York City before returning to Berkeley as a research associate.

As a founding member of the Creation Research Society, Dr. Gish met Dr. Henry Morris. A few years later, when Dr. Morris and Dr. Tim LaHaye founded Christian Heritage College and a research division in 1970, Dr. Gish accepted a position with the Institute for Creation Research, and served there as senior vice president for many years. Today, he is senior vp emeritus, and continues his writing career. Dr. Gish is a prolific author—among his classics are *Evolution: The Fossils Still Say No!*—and is a legendary debater, challenging evolutionary scientists in dozens of forums.